Philip Hewitt

Training
Englische Grammatik
9./10. Schuljahr

Lösungsheft

Ernst Klett Verlag
Stuttgart Düsseldorf Leipzig

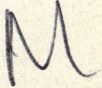

Kapitel 1

Einstufungstest

1b), 2a), 3a), 4c), 5c), 6b), 7c), 8c), 9b), 10a)

Training 1

a) *Adverbs*

1. with verbs:

goes <u>well</u> — will be lowered <u>gently</u> — flies <u>faster</u> than — can move as <u>fast</u> as — leap <u>vertically</u> — are <u>gradually</u> being explored — <u>easily</u> contain — will <u>far</u> outweigh — will benefit <u>immediately</u>

2. with adjectives:

<u>equally</u> great — <u>Majestically</u> moving

3. with other adverbs:

<u>much</u> more ... than — <u>fairly</u> regularly

b) *Adjectives*

the <u>last</u> frontier — <u>next</u> year — a <u>revolutionary new</u> submarine — <u>first</u> voyage — <u>Deep</u> Flight I — <u>other deep-sea</u> research vessels — the ... <u>highest</u> mountain — <u>manned</u> voyages ... have become <u>common</u> — the <u>deepest</u> parts — <u>Deep</u> Flight I — are <u>most interested</u> in — the <u>deepest</u> parts — <u>little</u> is known about the <u>middle</u> waters — the ... <u>last great</u> frontier — <u>more</u> life by weight — <u>other</u> ecosystem — their <u>eco-nomic</u> potential is equally <u>great</u> — <u>moving</u> ocean currents — <u>weather-related</u> disasters — <u>many valuable</u> minerals and <u>other</u> substances — discoveries <u>helpful</u> to

Training 2

Alternativen werden durch Schrägstriche (/) gekennzeichnet.

1. the *Trieste* was <u>carefully</u> lowered/lowered <u>carefully</u> to — 2. two <u>brave</u> scientists. — 3. behaved <u>well.</u> — 4. the <u>complicated</u> vehicles; <u>only</u> contained/contained <u>only</u> the passengers. — 5. They went down <u>very slowly</u>. — 6. They reached the bottom <u>safely</u>. — 7. They <u>soon</u> knew/that men would <u>soon</u> be able ... — 8. After the ... <u>dramatic</u> dive,/... increased <u>dramatically</u>. — 9. The <u>old</u> American — 10. vehicles <u>remotely</u> operated/operated <u>remotely</u> from; <u>quickly</u> followed/followed <u>quickly</u>.— 11. equipped with <u>expensive</u> cameras/These were <u>expensively</u> equipped — 12. for <u>scientific</u> research./others were <u>scientifically</u> designed for research. — 13. <u>marine</u> biologists — 14. A <u>completely</u> new era — 15. an <u>imperfect</u> basic know-ledge — 16. an <u>endless</u>, flat plain stretching/a flat plain stretching <u>endlessly</u> from — 17. when <u>closely</u> examined/examined <u>closely</u> — 18. <u>astonishingly deep</u>.

Training 3

Across: 5. useful — 6. quickly — 8. unhappy — 9. far — 12. carefully — 14. first — 15. fully

Down: 1. slowly — 2. well — 3. quick — 4. loud — 7. sure — 10. full — 11. early — 13. awful

15.6.04

Training 4

1. <u>good</u> snack-bar; really <u>well</u>; <u>better</u> than; the <u>best</u> place — 2. be <u>worse</u> than; the <u>worst</u> salads; doing <u>badly</u> — 3. <u>more interesting</u> than — 4. was <u>happy</u>; is <u>happier</u> than; the <u>happiest</u> people; very <u>happy</u> — 5. find it <u>more difficult</u> than; it's <u>less difficult</u> than; the <u>most difficult</u> language — 6. have <u>much</u> time; had <u>more</u> time; as <u>much</u> money; <u>many</u> hobbies; <u>more</u> carefully — 7. have <u>less</u> time; has a <u>little</u> time; watches <u>less</u> than; watches the <u>least</u> of all — 8. feel <u>good</u> today; feel <u>better</u> than; would be <u>best</u>; work <u>better</u>; do <u>better</u>; did so <u>badly</u>; my <u>worst</u> exams; won't do <u>well</u>; will be <u>worse</u> than — 9. <u>extreme</u> views; <u>extremely</u> strict; <u>more extreme</u> than; the <u>most extreme</u> headmaster

Training 5 ✗

Lösungsvorschlag:

1. The weather was very <u>bright</u> when we arrived in the Scottish Highlands. The sun was shining <u>brightly</u>.
2. We were very <u>happy</u>. We cycled <u>happily</u> along/through the countryside.
3. We cycled <u>carefully</u> down a steep hill./We were very <u>careful</u> because the hill was very steep.
4. It was still very <u>early</u> when we arrived at Loch Ness./When we arrived at Loch Ness it was still very <u>early</u>.
5. We felt very <u>lazy</u>, so we lay <u>lazily</u> on the bank of the lake/Loch Ness in the sunshine.
6. <u>Suddenly</u> Nessie, the Loch Ness Monster, appeared./We <u>suddenly</u> saw Nessie, the Loch Ness Monster.
7. <u>Quickly</u> I/I <u>quickly</u> picked up my camera.
8. Nessie was swimming <u>calmly</u> on the surface of the loch/lake.
9. We were very <u>excited</u>. We got on our bikes and cycled <u>excitedly</u> to the office of the Inverness News.
10. <u>Unluckily</u> there was no film in the <u>camera!</u>/<u>Unluckily</u> I had forgotten to put a film in the camera. We had been very <u>unlucky</u>! (= *Wir hatten großes Pech gehabt.*) We were very <u>unhappy</u> (*nicht:* unlucky) about our bad <u>luck</u>!

Training 6

1. Adverb bzw. adverbiale Bestimmung am Satzanfang:
<u>Sometimes</u> there is high grass in a field — <u>Always</u> ask permission before you camp

2. Adverb bzw. adverbiale Bestimmung am Satz- oder Satzteilende:
it will be difficult for the farmer to cut the hay <u>later</u> — It is probably best to ask the farmer <u>first</u> — Dozens of sheep and lambs are killed <u>on British farms each year</u>

3. Adverb vor dem Hauptverb:
you should <u>always</u> observe The Country Code — You should <u>never</u> walk across fields — Most paths are <u>clearly</u> marked. — Farmers don't <u>usually</u> mind — if you <u>thoughtlessly</u> walk across this field — Farmers will not <u>often</u> refuse permission — even though they <u>almost always</u> charge a small sum — Dogs <u>often</u> run after other animals — A strange dog will <u>certainly</u> frighten farm animals and may <u>possibly</u> injure them

4. Adverbien der Art und Weise:
Follow them <u>carefully</u> — which a farmer has planted <u>specially</u> — their owners have not kept them <u>properly under control</u>

Folgendes Adverb passt nicht in eine der obigen Kategorien:
unless you are <u>perfectly</u> sure *(Adverb bestimmt Adjektiv)*

Training 7 ✗ 15.3.04

1. We often go to bed at ten o'clock./At ten o'clock we often ...
2. They have always lived in London.
3. Next year we are flying to Spain in the autumn.
4. Luckily he was not driving his car very fast.
5. She has never been to London in December.
6. I rarely watch TV at the weekends.
7. She only looked at it closely once./She only looked at it once closely.
8. Yesterday he nearly drove his new motor scooter into a wall./He … yesterday.
9. We regularly eat salad for lunch in summer./In summer we … for lunch.
10. Do you often come to the youth club on Fridays?
11. She walked across the room carefully in the dark./Carefully she walked …
12. They have often tried very hard to find work nearer home.
13. Tomorrow we're going to a football match in the afternoon.

Training 8 ✗ 8.3.04

1. When we arrived at the campsite it was terribly late.
2. But we had often stayed at this site before, so that was no problem.
3. We put up our tent unbelievably quickly and were in our sleeping bags soon afterwards.
4. About an hour later I woke up./I woke up about an hour later.
5. I could hear someone walking quietly around the campsite.

5

6. My friend Tom was snoring loudly beside me.
7. He was a heavy sleeper.
8. Perhaps the warden was quickly making a last check/... was making a last quick check before going happily to his own bed.
9. Then I heard very quiet voices.
10. A man and a woman were talking softly to each other.
11. "This is an absolutely impossible place!" said the man.
12. "We can't possibly put up our tent here in the middle of the night. People are trying to sleep!"
13. "If we had left early and arrived here before midnight everything would have been OK.
14. Now we'll have to get up early and ask the warden if we can stay. It's all your fault."
15. "Why is it always my fault?" asked the man. "You're the one who is so terribly keen on camping!"
16. "Be quiet!" whispered the woman. "You'll wake someone up."
17. They didn't know that they had already woken me up./ ... woken me up already.

Training 9

1. The CD sounded loud/terrible.
2. We looked carefully at the picture./... at the picture carefully.
3. She screamed terribly at the picture/when she saw my homework.
4. The explorers felt their way carefully along the tunnel.
5. Jackie gave a loud/terrible scream.
6. My teacher criticized me angrily/screamed terribly when she/he saw my homework.
7. The food smelt/tasted delicious/terrible/unusual.
8. The butler sounded the dinner gong loudly.
9. Her singing sounded beautiful/terrible.
10. I felt terrible after my flight./I gave a terrible scream.

Training 10

1. a high-flying aircraft — 2. a well-dressed girl — 3. a long-lasting battery — 4. a well-organized rock concert — 5. a badly-prepared lesson — 6. a sweet-smelling rose — 7. an attractive-looking girl — 8. a fast-moving vehicle — 9. a badly-scratched LP — 10. low-lying ground

Kapitel 2

Einstufungstest

1a), 2c, 3b), 4a), 5b), 6a), 7d), 8c), 9b), 10c)

Training 1

1. My mother is not working in an office at present/at the moment. (Ort vor Zeit!) —
2. Oliver and Tanja play tennis every week. — 3. Do you always go to school at half past seven? — 4. He's always playing his violin! — 5. They are learning Spanish now/at the moment. — 6. He doesn't speak English well/good English. — 7. Does she never go swimming? — 8. I don't play football. — 9. He rarely listens to jazz. — 10. Next week I'm going to a rock concert. — 11. The last bus leaves at midnight. — 12. What are you doing tomorrow?

Training 2

Simple form:
The Channel coast ... has some of the finest beaches *(kein Hilfsverb hier!)* — The White Cliffs of Dover stand guard — people who want to explore the countryside — Devon and Cornwall lie in the extreme south-west of England. — Visit Dartmoor and Exmoor, where ponies still live wild. — Cornwall possesses many interesting relics — (Cornwall) is still the home of china clay mining. *(kein Hilfsverb hier!)* — This is the Heart of England. *(kein Hilfsverb!)* — Every year many thousands of people visit the home of ... — Tourists love the mellow stone houses — which they find in the Cotswolds. — But the charm of the Cotswolds does not end with ... — Visitors come from all over Europe ... — Who says there is nothing to see ... — ... from the centre of Manchester lies some of England's prettiest moorland scenery. — It runs from Carlisle on the west coast to Newcastle ... and is the biggest single national monument in Britain.

Progressive form:
If you are planning a holiday with a difference — ... that are waiting to welcome you. — Are you thinking of spending longer than a week here? — Yorkshire ... and its capital, York ... are waiting to be discovered. — What are you waiting for? — We are looking forward to seeing you in England next year!

Modal auxiliaries:
You can explore the quiet country lanes in your own car. — Then you might like to rent one of the holiday flats — which are to be found in most of the larger towns. — Who could resist places which have names like ...

7

Training 3

1. aren't listening — 2. are you thinking — 3. go; we are going — 4. They're having — 5. They have — 6. are they staying — 7. have — 8. take — 9. are driving — 10. are they coming — 11. Do you know — 12. don't think — 13. does she live? — 14. she's staying — 15. Do you mean; always arrives/is always arriving — 16. believe; she's — 17. don't see — 18. are you; Do you — 19. owes; need

Training 4

Hier einige mögliche Ergänzungen:

Dear Penfriend,
My name is … and I live in …
1. I often/seldom watch TV/read a book in the evenings.
2. At the moment I am writing to you!
3. I am fifteen years old/a fan of techno music.
4. Sometimes my family (and I) go out for a meal/go for a walk in the countryside.
5. Every week we/I visit our/my friends in …
6. We are usually at home on Sundays.
7. On Saturdays we never go to school/always go shopping.
8. I never forget to do my homework.
9. During the week we usually have lunch at home.
10. The sun is shining/I'm listening to the radio just now.

Training 5

2. a) "Are you going (to go) to London next week?"
   b) "(Please) Will you buy me a souvenir?"
3. a) "Shall I open the window?" — b) "Will the noise of traffic be too loud?"
4. a) "Aren't you going to offer me a sweet?"
   b) "You'll have a stomach-ache if you eat them all!"
5. a) "OK, I'll go!" — b) "Aren't you going to answer the door?"
6. a) "Shall we start again?" — b) "We won't have enough time."

Training 6

a) "I'm not going to get involved." — b) "I'm not going to stop." — c) "Nobody will see me if I walk away." — d) "Someone will arrive in a few minutes. I'll be late for school if I wait any longer!" — e) "Shall I call a doctor?" — f) "Stay here! I'm going to call a doctor!" — g) "OK, I'll stay here." — h) "I hope she will be/she is going to be OK." — i) "Shall we try and get her out?" — j) "I'm not going to move her." — k) "Will you call the police, too?" — l) "Yes, OK, I won't be long!"

Training 7

1. Sue will be travelling to Birmingham. — 2. John will be ironing his shirts. — 3. Mum will be reading the paper. — 4. Dad will be sitting in the garden. — 5. Julia will be washing her hair. — 6. The boys will be playing football. — 7. Our teacher will be teaching (us) English. — 8. Pat and Jean will be listening to the radio. — 9. Our cat will be having (its) lunch.

Training 8

1.+h. What will you do if you can't find the key? — 2.+e. What will you be doing this time next week? — 3.+g. Don't hit him or he'll tell the police! — 4.+b. Don't disturb him because he'll probably be sleeping. — 5.+j. Will they be having lunch when we arrive? — 6.+f. Will they have lunch before we arrive? — 7.+i. If we arrive late they will be having breakfast. — 8.+c. When we arrive we will all have breakfast. — 9.+a. She'll finish work at exactly ten past five. — 10.+d. She'll be finishing work about now.

Andere Kombinationen sind auch möglich, so z.B.:
1.+f. What will you do before we arrive?
2.+j. What will you be doing when we arrive?

Die alternativen Sätze bei 5 und 6 klingen allerdings dann etwas seltsam:
5.+e. Will they be having lunch this time next week?
6.+h. Will they have lunch if you can't find the key?

Training 9

1. will be waiting — 2. won't wait — 3. Will you listen — 4. Will you be listening — 5. What will you be doing; I'll be working — 6. What will you do; I'll work — 7. We'll be having tea — 8. We'll have tea — 9. I'll ask — 10. Will you be asking

Training 10

1. I will have passed my driving test. — 2. she will have finished her training. — 3. we will have been living/will have lived there for 10 years. — 4. will you have been learning English — 5. he'll have been talking — 6. He won't have been waiting — 7. he will have marked — 8. I'll have been saving — 9. I'll have saved enough — 10. Will they have arrived — 11. she will have been working — 12. she will have finished working — 13. they'll have finished building — 14. he'll have been studying English — 15. they'll have drunk

Kapitel 3

Einstufungstest

1c), 2b), 3a), 4a), 5c)

Training 1

A light rain <u>was falling</u> when I <u>reached</u> the station.
It was while I <u>was looking</u> for a seat that I <u>saw</u> her
… and as I <u>was watching</u> I suddenly <u>saw</u> a young man …
But the train <u>was travelling</u> quite fast now, so he <u>couldn't manage</u> to catch it.
Before five minutes <u>had passed</u>, Sheila and I <u>were talking</u> as if …
By the time we <u>were passing</u> through York, I <u>knew</u> that I had found myself a new girlfriend.
I <u>looked</u> up … and <u>saw</u> that Hilary <u>was walking</u> quickly …

Training 2

Background description:
I <u>was going</u> home after my first term at university, and I <u>was feeling</u> very happy.
I <u>was studying</u> in Edinburgh and still <u>living</u> with my parents
I <u>was</u> very much <u>looking</u> forward to going home
Many of my friends <u>were travelling</u> south on the same train,
The girl of my dreams <u>was sitting</u> there <u>reading</u> a paperback novel,
We <u>were</u> still <u>standing</u> at the platform.
Other young people <u>were putting</u> their bags … between the seats
He <u>was running</u> after the train.
She <u>was facing</u> the other way.
She <u>was</u> not <u>smiling</u>.

was …-ing = wollte
I <u>was keeping</u> this seat free for my boyfriend,
she <u>was staying</u> with an uncle and aunt over Christmas

One other progressive form is used. Did you write it down?
It is not a past progressive form, so don't worry if you didn't find it:
because my girlfriend Hilary <u>would be meeting</u> me at Kings Cross Station.

Training 3

1.+g. She was talking to me when the phone rang. — 2.+j. Before the robber entered the bank, she put a mask on. — 3.+i. When we went on holiday, we always locked all the doors. — 4.+a. John talked to Sheila when they met at the pub. — 5.+h. First they bought the tickets, then they got on the train. — 6.+d. While we were playing tennis, all our clothes were stolen. — <u>7.+b.</u> The boys grilled the meat while the girls were watching TV. — <u>8.+c.</u> When I last saw the bank robber, she was wearing a mask. — <u>9.+e.</u> They were on the platform when the train arrived. — <u>10.+f.</u> The boys were grilling the meat when the dog stole the sausages.

Training 4

1. waited — 2. were waiting — 3. did you say — 4. was talking — 5. was saying — 6. saw — 7. was doing — 8. was seeing — 9. talked — 10. did she do — 11. had — 12. was having

Training 5

1. While I was walking to school one morning, I saw an accident.
2. Just as I was crossing the road, a car drove into/hit another car.
3. When the police arrived, the two drivers were arguing/shouting at each other.
4. While the two policemen were just getting out of their car, one of the drivers hit the other driver.
5. While the driver who had been hit was lying on the ground, the other driver ran off.
6. Just as he was running round the corner, he ran into/hit a passer-by/a fat man who was coming round the other way.
7. While the driver was getting up, one of the policemen caught him.

Kapitel 4

Einstufungstest

1c), 2a), 3d), 4c), 5b), 6a), 7b), 8b)

Training 1

1. *Simple past – completed period of time is given or is clear from the context*
Violent confrontations between police and Asian youths <u>provoked</u> widespread shock last weekend.
The campaign <u>began</u> in Birmingham last year.
When repeated complaints ... <u>produced</u> no results, Asians <u>set up</u> vigilante groups to clean up the areas.
The violent confrontation with police in Bradford last weekend <u>showed</u> that ...

2. Present perfect – action still going on
Over the past few years Asians in Britain ... <u>have felt</u> very worried ...
... there <u>have been</u> many cases of crimes ...
A sex magazine with photos of Asian girls <u>has been</u> in circulation for over a year, ...
*This display of "civic responsibility" <u>has</u>, however, <u>involved</u> Muslims in the criticism ... that they are "anti-liberal".
*Young Asians <u>have taken over</u> the ... campaign ... and <u>made</u> it more militant.

3. Present perfect – action (or actions) completed at an undefined time in the past
... the way in which the wider culture ... <u>has invaded</u> the areas where they live.
Drug-taking <u>has increased</u> within the Asian community, ...
All this ... <u>has generated</u> a climate of moral panic.
*Many Asians living in city centres <u>have found</u> that the value of their houses goes down ...
Muslims <u>have started</u> a campaign to protect themselves ...
*This <u>has led</u> to a conflict of values and ways of life.
Many of them <u>have left</u> school without adequate qualifications, ...
... they <u>have adopted</u> Western values ...

4. Present perfect – action takes place in the present or very close to the present
a gay magazine for Asians <u>has</u> just <u>appeared</u>

*Die mit * gekennzeichneten Sätze in den Abschnitten 2 und 3 könnten auch im jeweils anderen Abschnitt eingeordnet werden.*

Training 2

Lösungsvorschläge:

play:
We played "hide and seek" as children. — I played "hide and seek" as a child. — Did you ever play "hide and seek" as a child? — Have you ever played football? — I/We often play football.

listen to:
Did you listen to the radio yesterday evening? — I/we listened to the radio yesterday evening. — We/I often listen to pop concerts on the radio. — I/We have never listened to pop concerts on the radio. — Have you ever listened to pop concerts on the radio?

visit:
Did you visit London last year? — We/I visited London last year. — Have you visited Frankfurt yet? — I/We have never visited Frankfurt. — We/I haven't visited Frankfurt yet.

eat:
Have you ever eaten fish and chips? — We/I have often eaten fish and chips. — Did you ever eat marmalade when you were in England? — I/We often ate marmalade when we were in England.

drink:
Did you ever drink beer when you were younger? — We/I never drank beer when we were/I was younger.

watch:
Did you watch a horror film on TV last night? — I watched a horror film on TV last night.

Training 3

Siehe Lösungsvorschläge oben. Dazu kommen folgende Fragen zu Gewohnheiten:
Do you often eat fish and chips? — Do you often play football?
Do you often listen to pop concerts on the radio?

Wenn es sich um mehrere Englandaufenthalte handelt, wäre auch die Frage möglich:
Have you often eaten marmalade when you were in England?

Training 4

26.4.04

1. has gone; went — 2. have lived; lived — 3. Did you do; Have you done — 4. did not drive; have not driven — 5. learnt; have not learnt — 6. wrote; has written — 7. have bought; bought — 8. Have you often drunk; Did you often drink — 9. Has Julie ever flown; did she fly — 10. Have you seen; Did you see

Training 5

1. We have seen this film twice. — 2. We saw this film last week. — 3. He lived/was living in Berlin when I knew him. — 4. My aunt works/is working in an office. — 5. My uncle has worked/has been working in England since 1990. — 6. Our teacher has visited/been to England three times. — 7. He has lived/has been living here for four years. — 8. He lived here for a year before he went/before going to the USA. — 9. She has just arrived. — 10. She always arrives punctually/on time.

Training 6

... the White Tower, <u>was</u> built by William the Conqueror ... <u>has been</u> used as a palace, a prison ... Many people <u>have been</u> imprisoned or executed ... including Anne Boleyn ... who <u>was</u> beheaded here ... Her ghost and many others <u>have been</u> seen

Training 7

1. has always had — 2. was; was — 3. worked; did not live; preferred — 4. was built — 5. was called; have taken over — 6. ran; was

Training 8

Jenny: Yes. I packed it yesterday. – Have you bought the food?
Paul: Yes/Of course. I bought it this afternoon. – (But) Have you packed your rucksack?
Jenny: I haven't finished (packing it) yet. I'm just doing/packing it.
or: Yes. I've just packed/finished packing it.
– Have you phoned the camp site (yet)?
Paul: Yes. I've just phoned them yesterday. (They're expecting us.)

Kapitel 5

Einstufungstest ✓ 22.3.04

1d), 2c), 3b), 4d), 5c)

Training 1

Present perfect simple:
We <u>have gained</u> the knowledge and expertise.
Emma and a team of eleven 17-year-olds <u>have mastered</u> the mysteries …
… the course <u>has</u> now <u>become</u> part of the school curriculum.
They <u>have</u> even <u>taken</u> British Rail's own … examination.
The station <u>has been</u> closed for 30 years.

Present perfect progressive:
… who <u>has been using</u> the station regularly …
The girls <u>have been providing</u> the kind of friendly service people want.
For the past year the girls <u>have been collecting</u> money …
… passengers from Whittington <u>have been having</u> to travel …

Training 2

1. Two years ago the station <u>was taken</u> over by girls …
2. Tickets worth £111,000 <u>were sold</u> …
3. … almost as much as <u>was taken</u> during the last year under British Rail.
4. … several thousand pounds <u>have</u> already <u>been collected</u>.

Training 3

1. because I've been playing football. — 2. even though she has been living in London for three years already. — 3. How long have you been waiting here? — 4. I think someone has been drinking it! — 5. We've been practising English grammar

14

since three o'clock. — 6. What has she been doing all afternoon? — 7. I've been looking forward to it all week! — 8. Has the baby been behaving well?

Training 4

1. Have you learnt — 2. have you been learning — 3. I haven't seen — 4. John has been seeing — 5. They have been having — 6. They have never had — 7. she has been working — 8. You have worked — 9. have you been doing … I've been listening — 10. have you done — 11. Have you been watching — 12. They have been watching — 13. Have you ever been

Training 5

Present perfect sentences:

1. John has been learning English/living here	
John has lived/has been working here	since last June.
2. We have been learning English/living here	
We have lived/been working here	for three years.
3. She has been learning English/living here	
She has lived/been working here	for six weeks.
4. They have been learning English/living here	
They have been working here	since they left Berlin.
5. Peter and Sophia have been learning English/living here	
Peter and Sofia have lived/been working here	since three months ago.

Simple past sentences:

5. John/We/She/They/	three years ago./
Peter and Sophia came/lived here	for six weeks.

Other answers are also possible, but not simple past tense + "since"

Training 6

1. For — 2. ago. — 3. since … since — 4. from — 5. Since — 6. For — 7. from — 8. ago — 9. since — 10. since

Training 7

1. … even though this service <u>has been running for</u> fifty years.
2. They say <u>that there has always been a bus service and that they have always used the buses</u>. One woman says <u>she has been using the bus since</u> 1958.
3. She is talking to some of the villagers. <u>"Have you written to the bus company?"</u> – "Yes, <u>but we haven't had/received a reply yet.</u>"
4. "Well, <u>we have decided to take over the bus service (ourselves)</u>.

5. I <u>have worked/been working on the buses since 1994</u>." – "Yes. I think I'm a good driver because <u>I've had a/my driving licence for 9 years</u>.
6. and <u>I've never had an accident/not had an accident yet</u>."
7. "The villagers of Strathdon <u>have been discussing the problem for two and a half hours</u>.
8. A representative of the bus company <u>has just arrived</u>. I'll try and have a few words with him after the meeting."
9. "Well, not really. We <u>have had a frank and open exchange of views</u> but no real progress <u>has been made</u>.
10. The bus company <u>has decided to let them try for (a period of) three weeks</u>."

Training 8

1. <u>Have</u> you <u>seen</u> my school-bag (anywhere)? — 2. <u>Have</u> you <u>been eating</u> my chocolate? — 3. Who <u>has eaten</u> (all) my chocolate? — 4. <u>Have</u> you <u>seen</u> Fred Smith recently? — 5. <u>Have</u> you <u>been waiting</u> (for me) long? — 6. How long <u>has</u> he <u>been living</u> here? — 7. Where on earth <u>have</u> you <u>been</u>? — 8. What <u>have</u> you <u>done</u>? — 9. What on earth <u>have</u> you <u>been doing</u>? — 10. Have you <u>been practising</u> English?

Kapitel 6

Einstufungstest

1a), 2b), 3b), 4c), 5a)

Training 1

1. <u>After</u> Patricia <u>had passed</u> her driving test, she bought a car.
2. <u>After</u> she <u>had driven</u> home, she locked the car.
3. <u>After</u> Patricia <u>had made</u> a cup of coffee, she phoned her friend Anna.
4. She put down the phone <u>after</u> she <u>had said</u> goodbye to Anna.
5. She looked out of the window <u>after</u> she <u>had heard</u> a loud noise.
6. Two young men were trying to steal her car radio <u>after</u> they <u>had broken</u> a window to get into the car.
7. <u>After</u> Patricia <u>had realized</u> what was happening, she rang the police.
8. Her neighbour came out of his house <u>after</u> he <u>had heard</u> the noise.
9. <u>After</u> the man <u>had shouted</u> something, the boys looked up and saw him.
10. <u>After</u> they <u>had run</u> away, a police car arrived outside Patricia's house.

Training 2

1.<u>When</u> he told me his name, I knew who he was. — 2. <u>When</u> we <u>had</u> finished lunch, we went for a walk. — 3. <u>When</u> she <u>had</u> wiped her feet on the doormat, she shut the front door. — 4. <u>When</u> he took the dog for a walk, it was very cold outside. — 5. <u>When</u> our teacher <u>had</u> given us the dictation, he collected our exercise books. — 6. My mum learnt Russian <u>when</u> she went to school in East Germany. — 7. <u>When</u> the sun <u>had</u> set, the stars came out. — 8. I lit a match <u>when</u> the lights went out. — 9. <u>When</u> he tried to speak French, everybody laughed. — 10. <u>When</u> all my friends were on holiday, I felt very lonely.

Training 3

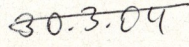

1. After we <u>had flown</u> from London to New York, we booked into a hotel in Manhattan. — 2. After we <u>had been</u> on/<u>had taken</u> a sightseeing trip round Manhattan, we went to see the Statue of Liberty. — 3. After we <u>had celebrated</u> Independence Day in New York City, we went by car/drove to Washington. — 4. After/When we <u>had seen</u> the sights of Washington, we went/flew/drove to Disneyworld in Orlando, Florida. — 5. After/When we <u>had spent</u> two days in Florida, we flew to Arizona. — 6. After/When we <u>had visited</u> the Grand Canyon, we went to/visited Yosemite National Park. 7. After/When we <u>had driven</u> over the Rockies to San Francisco, we stayed with friends there. — 8. After/When we <u>had seen</u> the Golden Gate Bridge and the other sights, we flew on to Seattle. — 9. After/When we <u>had spent</u> two days in Seattle with friends of Alan's, we flew back to London via Chicago. — 10. After/When we <u>had recovered</u> from the jet lag, we felt much better!

Training 4

1. <u>Before</u> he <u>had finished</u> his lunch, his guests arrived. — 1. He (had) finished his lunch <u>before</u> his guests arrived. — 2. She bought a newspaper <u>before</u> the train left.— 3. We put warm clothes on <u>before</u> we went out into the snow. — 4. The boy jumped off <u>before</u> the bus <u>had stopped</u>. — 5. The TV programme started <u>before</u> we <u>had finished</u> our homework. *or:* <u>Before</u> the TV programme started, we finished our homework. — 6. We <u>had reached</u> home <u>before</u> it began to rain. — 7. <u>Before</u> they <u>had reached</u> the bus station, the bus left. — 8. She left school <u>before</u> she <u>had finished</u> her course. — 9. They left New York <u>before</u> they <u>had had</u> time to see the Statue of Liberty. — 10. <u>Before</u> we <u>had started</u> to eat, the others arrived. *or:* We started to eat <u>before</u> the others <u>had arrived</u>.

Training 5

Einige Beispiele:

When:
When they met, they <u>fell</u> in love./They <u>fell</u> in love when they met.
When they moved to London, they <u>lived</u> in a small flat.
When they moved to London, they <u>found</u> a nice house.
When they got married, they <u>had known</u> each other for three years.

After:
After they <u>had met/known</u> each other for three years, they fell in love/They fell in love after they <u>had met/known</u> each other for three years.
After they <u>had known</u> each other for three years, they got married.
After they <u>had moved</u> to London, they lived in a small flat.
After they <u>had found</u> a nice house, they moved to London.

Before:

a) Erste Handlung **noch nicht fertig,** *als zweite anfängt:*
They got married before they <u>had found</u> a new house.
They moved to London before they <u>had got married</u>.
They got married before they <u>had known</u> each other for three years.
They moved to London before they <u>had found</u> a new house.
They fell in love before they <u>had found</u> a new house.

b) Erste Handlung **fertig,** *bevor zweite anfängt:*
They knew each other for three years before they <u>fell</u> in love.
They got married before they <u>moved</u> to London.
They lived in a small flat before they <u>found</u> a new house.
They found a new house before they <u>got</u> married.

Training 6

Johnny Brown, the famous pop singer, was born in 1970. After he <u>had left</u> school in 1985, he started work as an assistant in a music shop. When he <u>had been learning</u> to play the guitar for three years, he joined the Steve Miller Band, which he left after he <u>had</u> only <u>been playing</u> for two months. After he <u>had been living</u> in New York for three years, he founded The Konks. When the group <u>had been playing</u> together for two years, it broke up. After he <u>had solved</u> his drug problem, he founded a new group The Daws. Their first concert was so successful that they could only leave the stage after they <u>had given</u> six encores. They made their first CD in 1994 after their fans <u>had been waiting/(had waited)</u> for two years! The group <u>had been working</u> together for three years when they broke up in 1996. They <u>had given</u> twenty concerts and made three CDs.

Training 7

a) *Indirect speech*:
(Ralph ... had told him that) they had had lots of adventures. — (One of the gang had told him that) the house had been haunted ever since! — "Mum said I couldn't go out until I had finished my homework."

Unreal past:
run like hell before the vicar had had time to open the door! — as though they, not Mike, had been surprised by the ghost. — as if someone had heard the knocking.

b) *Real past*:
Mike had only been living in the village for a couple of weeks — when some of the boys ... had asked him ... — he had had to leave all his friends in the town — where he had lived all his life — so he was very pleased that he had been invited to join the gang. — Ralph ... had told him that ...— No problem, he had thought with a smile. — But he had never been to the Old Vicarage before — a building that had not been lived in for twenty years. — Not since the old vicar had died. — One of the other boys in the gang had told him that ... — Mike had not believed in Father Christmas — since he had woken late one Christmas Eve — The other members of the gang had been waiting in the bushes — Alan had been told that he should be — Mike had reached the front door now. — The moment had come. — Mike had knocked again. Slow footsteps had begun to walk towards the front door — Mike had not moved. — It had been locked years ago

Training 8

1. After he had eaten something, he went out for a little walk.
2. He had run home as if/as though the devil had been chasing him!
3. If he had seen me, he would certainly have stayed.
4. They bought the CD after they had heard it a couple of times.
5. She looked at me as if/as though I had gone mad.
6. They behaved as if/as though they had won the competition already!
   – I wish I'd been there!
7. He would have helped me if I had asked him.
8. Tom only cleared up his room after his mother had asked him twice.
9. If they had listened to me, they would be millionaires today!
10. My little brother came into my room, went (up) to my cupboard and took out the packet of biscuits as if/as though he had known it was hidden there!

Kapitel 7

Einstufungstest

1a), 2a), 3c), 4c), 5b), 6d), 7b), 8d), 9c), 10b)

Training 1

1. I <u>will</u> visit New York. — 2. if you <u>invite</u> us. — 3. we<u>'ll have</u> the barbecue outside. — 4. unless we <u>pick</u> them <u>up</u> at the airport/<u>fetch</u> them from the airport. — 5. if I <u>give</u> it you back on Tuesday? — 6. you <u>will not/won't enjoy</u> this book. — 7. <u>Will</u> you <u>help</u> me … if I help you in the garden? — 8. if I<u>'ve saved</u> enough money by then. — 9. Unless you <u>call</u> the police, the robbers <u>will escape</u>! — 10. Unless we <u>run</u> faster, the bull <u>will catch</u> us!

Training 2

1. may/might/can — 2. could — 3. could — 4. should — 5. may/might — 6. must/have to — 7. might — 8. needn't — 9. can — 10. mustn't/shouldn't

Training 3

<u>1.+e)</u> If the ferry sinks, we'll have to swim. — <u>2.+d)</u> Unless you behave, I won't let you go to the party. — <u>3.+a)</u> If you stole a car, you would be punished. — <u>4.+f)</u> If our teacher is ill, we won't have a test tomorrow. — <u>5.+b)</u> If the plane crashed, we'd all be killed. — <u>6.+c)</u> If the school burned down, we wouldn't be sorry. — <u>7.+i)</u> Will you phone me if you have time? — <u>8.+g)</u> Would you help them if you knew the number? — <u>9.+j)</u> She'll lend you her book if you ask nicely. — <u>10.+h)</u> I'd be more careful if I were you!

Training 4

Deine Ergänzungen sind dir frei überlassen, müssen aber die richtigen Zeitformen (s. oben) enthalten.

Training 5

1. will probably live — 2. knew — 3. is done — 4. Would … be — 5. will find — 6. were given — 7. will feel — 8. think — 9. are not/aren't trusted — 10. would … trust

Training 6

Type I:

If you <u>stand</u> around a London Underground station for long enough you <u>will</u> probably <u>witness</u> at least one case of mugging.

If you <u>study</u> the few statistics available you <u>will find</u> that …

These … questions <u>will</u> still <u>have to be</u> answered if a solution to street crime <u>is</u> to be found.

<u>Should</u> you <u>try</u> to stop a mugging if you <u>see</u> one happening?

Type II:

But how <u>would</u> you <u>define</u> mugging if someone <u>asked</u> you …

If he <u>were</u> only <u>talking</u> about Central London, he <u>would</u> probably <u>be</u> right.

… in this area <u>would</u>, if <u>asked</u>, <u>describe</u> their attackers as "black".

… a mugging <u>would tend</u> not to be reported … <u>were</u> involved.

Type III:

If he <u>had thought</u> more carefully, … he <u>would not have caused</u> such a furore.

Others:

… a black <u>is</u> less likely to report … if he <u>is mugged</u> by another black *(Regelbox 6)*

… if they <u>had been</u>, you <u>would</u> probably still <u>find</u> that mugging is …*(Regelbox 5)*

Training 7

2. If he had bought new tyres, he wouldn't have had a puncture. — 3. If he hadn't had a puncture, he wouldn't have got wet. — 4. If he hadn't got wet, he wouldn't have caught a cold. — 5. If he hadn't caught a cold, he wouldn't have moved into the Bed and Breakfast place. — 6. If he hadn't moved into the Bed and Breakfast place, he wouldn't have met Claire. — 7. If he hadn't met Claire, he wouldn't have climbed the hill. — 8. If he hadn't climbed the hill, he wouldn't have hurt his ankle. — 9. If he hadn't hurt his ankle, his holiday wouldn't have been spoilt.

Training 8

1. like — 2. will give — 3. had lived — 4. would you do — 5. won't/will not be able — 6. saved — 7. would never have been captured — 8. find — 9. will not kill — 10. were

Training 9

1. <u>If</u> the Titanic <u>had not sunk</u>, it <u>could have/might have become</u> a floating museum. — 2. He <u>could have/might have become</u> rich if he <u>had not lost</u> all his money. — 3. The Loch Ness monster <u>could have been</u> put in a museum if it <u>had been caught</u>. — 4. John Smith <u>might not have lost</u> his job if he <u>had worked</u> hard. — 5. If Edison <u>had not invented</u> the light bulb, he <u>could have/might have died</u> poor. — 6. She <u>might not/would not have helped</u> her boyfriend if she <u>had known</u> he was a criminal. — 7. If

Scotland <u>had not become</u> part of Great Britain in 1707, it <u>might have/could have</u> <u>remained</u> a separate kingdom. / Scotland <u>would not/could not have become</u> part of Great Britain in 1707 if it <u>had remained</u> a separate kingdom. — 8. If President Kennedy <u>had not been assassinated</u>, Lyndon B. Johnson <u>would not/might not have</u> <u>become</u> President of the USA. — 9. If you <u>had had</u> a car, you <u>could have driven</u> to the seaside. — 10. My uncle <u>might/would not have had</u> a heart attack if his car had not been stolen.

Training 10

1. If I <u>had won</u> a prize, I <u>wouldn't be</u> unhappy. — 2. John <u>wouldn't be living</u> in London now if he <u>hadn't found</u> a job there last year. — 3. If my friend <u>hadn't started</u> learning French a couple of years ago, he <u>wouldn't spend</u> his holidays there regularly. — 4. If you <u>liked</u> the group's last CD, you<u>'ll love</u> this one — 5. You <u>won't know</u> Alice if you <u>weren't</u> at my party last year. — 6. If he <u>hadn't emigrated</u> to Australia when he was a boy, he <u>wouldn't be</u> a wealthy farmer now. — 7. If she <u>hadn't learned</u> to speak Arabic when she was a girl, she <u>wouldn't be working</u> in Beirut now. — 8. If you <u>bought</u> your mountain bike three years ago, you <u>will need</u> a new one now! — 9. How <u>will</u> you <u>recognize</u> him if you<u>'ve</u> never <u>seen</u> him before? — 10. "If they <u>have</u> never <u>been</u> there, they <u>won't know</u> the place."

Training 11

1. If she <u>says</u> no, he <u>says</u> yes. — 2. If you <u>will</u> just <u>wait</u> outside, I'm sure he'll be here in a minute. — 3. If you <u>should want</u> to come, please phone me. *or:* <u>Should</u> you <u>want</u> to come, please phone me. — 4. <u>Had</u> I <u>known</u> he was here, I would have invited him in. — 5. If you <u>would ask</u> her to help me with my homework, I'd be very grateful. — 6. If he<u>'d like</u> to borrow my book, I'll lend it to him. — 7. There's always an argument if they <u>can't</u> agree what to do. — 8. <u>Should</u> you <u>change</u> your mind, please let me know. — 9. I would have been able to help, <u>had</u> I <u>known</u> the answer. — 10. <u>Should</u> you (ever) <u>need</u> money, just phone me.

Training 12

1. If I <u>give</u> Tom your message, you<u>'ll/you will see</u> him tonight./If I <u>gave</u> Tom your message, you<u>'d/you would see</u> him tonight. — 2. If you/I/we etc. <u>had</u> not <u>left</u> London last year, you/I/we etc. <u>would not/wouldn't be</u> here now. — 3. If he <u>weren't/were not</u> a champion boxer, I<u>'d/I would punch</u> his nose./If he <u>had/he'd been</u> a champion boxer, I <u>wouldn't/would not have punched</u> … — 4. You (don't) <u>get</u> ice-cream if you <u>freeze</u> milk. — 5. If you <u>would</u> please <u>stop</u> talking, I<u>'ll explain</u> everything. — 6. If I/he/she etc. <u>had had</u> enough money, I/he/she etc. <u>would have gone</u> to America last year. — 7. If you <u>need</u> money now, I <u>will/I'll lend</u> you £50./If you <u>needed</u> money now, I <u>would/I'd lend</u> you £50. — 8.If you/he/they etc. <u>had worked</u> harder then, you etc. <u>would be</u>

happier now. — 9. You <u>would get</u> a job if you <u>lived</u> nearer the factory./You <u>would have got</u> a job if you <u>had lived</u> nearer the factory. — 10. If I <u>were</u> younger, I <u>would emigrate</u> to New Zealand.

Training 13

1. We can have a break when this exercise is over. — 2. She'll pass her exams if they aren't too hard. — 3. I might go to Venezuela if my dad pays my fare. — 4. You should talk to Jean if you want to learn French. — 5. They could go to Spain if Mr Johnson went with them. — 6. We can get married when I have enough money. — 7. She'd get a better job if she could speak Spanish. — 8. I have no idea when he'll be arriving. — 9. You'll remember him when you see him next.

Kapitel 8

Einstufungstest

1d), 2b), 3d), 4c), 5a), 6a), 7d), 8d), 9c), 10c)

Training 1

1. Yesterday Kate's mother <u>asked her to go</u> to the shop and buy her a kilo of rice and a few other things.
2. Her little brother Tommy <u>begged her to take</u> him to the shop with her.
3. Kate agreed but <u>warned/told him not to ask</u> for any sweets.
4. In the shop Kate <u>told/warned Tommy not to touch</u> anything.
5. Then Tommy <u>wanted/asked Kate to buy him</u> an ice lolly, but Kate said no.
6. Tommy started to cry, but Kate <u>begged him not to cry</u> in the shop.
7. After that, Kate <u>told Tommy/her brother to wait</u> for her at the cash desk.
8. The shopkeeper <u>warned an old lady/shouted to an old lady to look out</u>.
9. Then the shopkeeper <u>requested Kate to leave</u> his shop.
10. Outside, Kate <u>ordered/told Tommy never to do</u> that again.

Training 2

1. The teacher/My mother/... asked us/me/... to stop talking.
2. The teacher/farmer/policeman/... ordered/told him/her/me/us/... to empty his/her/my/our/... pockets.
3. The captain ordered/commanded the crew/passengers to abandon (the) ship.
4. The policeman/detective told/ordered the taxi-driver/motorist to follow that/the bank-robbers' car.

5. The salesman/saleswoman advised/recommended the customer to wash this/that/the T-shirt in lukewarm water only.   *or:* ... only to wash ... water.
6. My/His/Her/The boy's mother/father told me/him/her not to hit my/his/her sister.
7. The driving instructor/teacher told/warned/advised his/her pupil to always look over his/her shoulder when reversing.
8. The PE teacher warned/told the pupils never to come into the gym ...
9. Our maths teacher/... ordered/shouted at/told us to shut up and sit down.
10. I/He/She/... asked him/her/me/... to meet me/him/her/... at the station.
11. The advertisement/poster recommended people/readers/passers-by to buy ....
12. He/She/I/... begged me/her/him/... not to drive so fast.
13. The policeman/bank-robber told/ordered the people/us/me/... to put up their/our/my/... hands and (to) stand perfectly still.
14. The soldier/officer commanded/ordered the gunner/soldiers to fire.
15. Our teacher/... begged us to pay attention.

Training 3

a) 1. He/She says he/she <u>lives</u> in a flat. — 2. He/She says he/she <u>likes</u> techno. — 3. He/She says he/she <u>has</u> got two brothers and a sister. — 4. He/She says his/her hobbies <u>are</u> football and skateboarding. — 5. He/She says he/she <u>plays</u> in a club. — 6. He/She says he/she <u>doesn't</u> go to school on Saturdays any more. — 7. He/She says he/she <u>hasn't been</u> to America yet. — 8. He/She says he/she only <u>started</u> English a year ago. — 9. He/She says he/she <u>likes</u> it over here. — 10. He/She says he/she <u>is</u> going back to Germany in two weeks. — 11. He/She says he/she <u>was</u> playing football. — 12. He/She says she/the girl <u>is</u> Elke and that she <u>comes</u> from Dortmund, too. He/She says she <u>came</u> to the park after she <u>had done</u> her homework.

b) 1. He/She said he/she <u>lived</u> in a flat. — 2. He/She said he/she <u>liked</u> techno. — 3. He/She said he/she <u>had</u> got two brothers and a sister. — 4. He/She said his/her hobbies <u>were</u> football and skateboarding. — 5. He/She said he/she <u>played</u> in a club. — 6. He/She said he/she <u>didn't</u> go to school on Saturdays any more. — 7. He/She said he/she <u>hadn't been</u> to America yet. — 8. He/She said he/she <u>had</u> only <u>started</u> English a year ago. — 9. He/She said he/she <u>liked</u> it over here. — 10. He/She said he/she <u>was</u> going back to Germany in two weeks. — 11. He/She said he/she <u>had been</u> playing football. — 12. He/She said she/the girl <u>was</u> Elke and that she <u>came</u> from Dortmund, too. He/She said she <u>had come</u> to the park after she <u>had done</u> her homework.

Training 4

24.5.04

1. a) She said (that) she <u>was</u> staying <u>here tonight</u>. — b) She told me yesterday morning she <u>was</u> staying <u>here for the night/on Sunday night</u>. — c) On Sunday she informed me that she <u>was</u> staying <u>there/in Leeds for the night/on Sunday night</u>.

2. a) Peter told me that he <u>had seen</u> John <u>here on Monday/the day before yesterday</u>.
   b) Peter told me that he <u>had seen</u> John <u>in London on Monday</u>.
   c) Peter rang me and said that he <u>had seen</u> John <u>here yesterday</u>.
3. a) A friend recommended me to come <u>to Ireland</u> for my holiday <u>this year</u>.
   b) John advised me to go <u>to Ireland</u> for my holiday <u>next year</u>.
   c) I was advised to go <u>to Ireland</u> for my holiday <u>last year</u>.

Training 5

1. Our teacher told us (that) he <u>had</u> to go and see the headmaster, <u>so</u> he asked us <u>to take</u> out our books and do the exercise on page 23. or: Our teacher asked us <u>to take</u> out our books … <u>because</u> he <u>had</u> to go and see the headmaster. — 2. My mother asked me <u>to give</u> her my old jeans <u>because</u> she <u>wanted</u> to wash them. — 3. My brother told me/said he <u>had lent</u> me £2 and asked me <u>to give</u> it him back. — 4. My sister told me <u>to take</u> that/the T-shirt off <u>because</u> it <u>was</u> hers. — 5. My friend asked me <u>to have</u> another biscuit and told me/<u>because</u> he <u>had</u> got plenty. — 6. The/A policeman told/warned us that the/this road <u>had been flooded</u> and asked us <u>to follow</u> the DIVERSION signs. — 7. My uncle asked me <u>to come</u> in and <u>sit</u> down. Then he asked me <u>to have</u> a cup of tea and said/told me that/<u>because</u> he <u>hadn't been</u> expecting me so early. — 8. The inspector told me that the/this ticket <u>was</u> only valid with a Young Person's Railcard, <u>so</u> he asked me to show him my Railcard. — 9. My/Her ex-boyfriend told me/her <u>to go</u> home <u>because</u> he <u>hadn't invited</u> me/her to his party. — 10. The notice advised us <u>to avoid</u> the last-minute rush and <u>to post</u> early for Christmas. *or:* …to avoid the last-minute rush <u>by posting</u> early for Christmas.

Training 6

a) 1. I want to know if this exercise is difficult./… if the water is warm enough for swimming. — 2. She wanted to find out whether she could get a bus to Chelsham. — 3. He asked me if I knew the right answer. — 4. Our teacher sometimes asks if we do our homework on the bus. — 5. The man asked her whether she had seen his umbrella. — 6. My mother wants to know if this exercise is difficult./… if you'll be staying for supper. — 7. The driver inquired whether the hotel had a good garage. — 8. He wondered if his parents knew where he was. — 9. They wanted to know if their son had received their letter yet. — 10. I wonder whether the water is warm enough for swimming.

b) 1. "Is this exercise difficult?" / "Is the water warm enough for swimming?" — 2. "Can I get a bus to Chelsham?" — 3. "Do you know the right answer?" — 4. "Do you do your homework on the bus?" — 5. "Have you seen my umbrella?" — 6. "Is this exercise difficult?"/"Will he/she/your friend be staying for supper?" — 7. "Does the hotel have/Has the hotel got a good garage?" — 8. "Do my parents know where I am?" — 9. "Has our son/Have you received our letter yet?" — 10. "Is the water warm enough for swimming?"

Training 7

1. My father asked me who <u>had left</u> the front door open. — 2. She wants to know what (on earth) we <u>are doing</u> here. — 3. His friend asked her how much money <u>she had (got)</u>. — 4. The reporter requested information about how many prisoners <u>had escaped</u> before the prison staff <u>had found</u> the hole. — 5. He wants to know when the football match <u>took</u> place. — 6. The motorist asked the mechanic how soon he <u>could</u> repair his car. — 7. Our youth leader wanted to know what <u>had happened</u> to John. — — 8. One of the tourists has just asked me how far Reading <u>is</u> from London. — 9. The child asked his mother where flies <u>went</u> in the winter. — 10. The detective asked me what I <u>had done</u> after I had left the hotel.

Training 8

1. The sergeant <u>ordered</u> the soldier <u>to wake up, asking him</u> what <u>was</u> the matter with him. — 2. Ken <u>said</u> he loved French wine, and <u>asked</u> Peter <u>to pass him</u> the bottle. — 3. Peter <u>asked if/whether</u> Patrick <u>liked</u> wine, too, and <u>suggested that they should offer/suggested offering</u> him some. — 4. The wife <u>told</u> her husband that he <u>didn't</u> pay attention <u>to her and that she had to</u> tell him everything twice. — 5. Tania <u>ordered/commanded</u> her dog Robin <u>to come to her, asking him</u> where <u>he had got</u> those sausages and <u>saying that he was</u> a bad dog. — 6. The manager of the firm <u>asked</u> the young lady <u>if she was</u> Janet Smith. <u>When she said she was, he asked her to come</u> in and <u>sit</u> down. <u>Then he offered her</u> a cigarette/<u>asked her if she wanted</u> a cigarette. — 7. Angela <u>told</u> her boyfriend Derek <u>that she had been</u> surprised not to see <u>him</u> at Phil's party. <u>She asked him</u> where <u>he had been the previous night, warning him/and warned him to tell her</u> the truth. — 8. Oliver <u>suggested that we wait/suggested waiting</u> a few minutes longer. <u>He told me he had</u> no idea where the others <u>had</u> got to, <u>and asked me whether I thought</u> they <u>were</u> lost. — 9. The driving instructor <u>told</u> my sister/brother <u>to stop, saying he/she had run</u> over a hen <u>and asking why he/she couldn't drive</u> more carefully. — 10. My teacher <u>suggested that we should finish/suggested finishing</u> this exercise and <u>have/having</u> a break. <u>I said that was</u> a good idea.

Training 9

1. *Reporter:* When <u>did</u> you <u>start</u> to take ecstasy?
   Sarah: It <u>was</u> at a party.
   Reporter: What <u>made</u> you start?
   Sarah: Everyone else at the party <u>was taking</u> something. I <u>felt</u> a bit of an outsider.
   Reporter: <u>Have</u> you ever <u>tried</u> any other drugs?
   Sarah: A friend <u>offered</u> me a joint last week, but I <u>refused</u> it.
   Reporter: <u>Do</u> you <u>think</u> you <u>will want</u> to try stronger drugs now?
   Sarah: No. Ecstasy <u>gives</u> me all I need.

2. *Reporter:* How long <u>have</u> you <u>been selling</u> drugs, Darrel?
   Darrel: I <u>started</u> while I was still at school. I<u>'ve been selling</u> ecstasy and other tablets for about three years now.
   Reporter: <u>Don't</u> you <u>have</u> a bad conscience about exploiting young people?
   Darrel: No. I <u>know</u> that the tablets I<u>'m selling are</u> good quality stuff.
   Reporter: <u>How much do</u> these tablets <u>cost</u>?
   Darrel: That <u>depends</u> on what each customer <u>wants</u>.
   Reporter: <u>What do</u> you <u>mean</u>?
   Darrel: Some of the kids <u>like</u> to mix ecstasy with LSD and cocaine.
   Reporter: <u>Don't</u> you <u>think</u> taking cocaine is the way into the hard drugs scene?
   Darrel: Perhaps it is. It's a risk the kids have to take.

3. *Reporter:* <u>How did</u> your daughter <u>get</u> involved in drugs?
   Mrs Tate: Sheila <u>began</u> with dance drugs like ecstasy.
   Reporter: <u>How</u> old <u>was</u> she when she <u>started</u>?
   Mrs Tate: Sheila <u>was</u> only fourteen. My husband and I <u>were</u> horrified when she <u>was brought</u> home early one morning in an ambulance.
   Reporter: <u>Weren't</u> you <u>able to/Couldn't</u> you <u>stop</u> her? She was only fourteen, after all.
   Mrs Tate: We <u>tried,</u> but the attraction of drugs <u>was</u> stronger. All her friends <u>were</u> on drugs.
   Reporter: <u>What happened</u> after that?
   Mrs Tate: She <u>went</u> from ecstasy and LSD to cocaine and heroin. She<u>'s having</u> medical treatment at a drugs centre at the moment. Sheila's addiction <u>broke</u> up our marriage. My ex-husband still <u>blames</u> me for what <u>has happened</u> to our only child.

Kapitel 9

Einstufungstest

1c), 2c), 3b), 4b), 5c), 6a), 7c), 8a), 9b), 10b) ✗

Training 1

1. interested in; very interesting — 2. frightening experience; frightened of — 3. boiling water; hard-boiled eggs — 4. falling rain; fallen leaves — 5. fully booked; booking-office — 6. be terrified of; nothing terrifying about — 7. worn out

✗

Training 2

many people <u>living</u> in London — Cockney was the dialect <u>spoken</u> by people <u>born</u> in the East End — the bells of St Mary-le-Bow (<u>known</u> as Bow Bells) — Foreigners <u>listening</u> to a real Cockney — A Cockney <u>saying</u>: ... — Cockneys <u>educated</u> at grammar schools — someone less well <u>educated</u>

Training 3

1. The man <u>standing</u> — 2. The one <u>wearing</u> — 3. The one <u>dressed</u> — 4. the man <u>wanted</u> by — 5. the man <u>living</u> in — 6. that bank <u>situated</u> — 7. the one <u>invited</u> to — 8. one of the men <u>working</u> at — 9. a name <u>beginning</u> with Mac — 10. that chain of restaurants <u>selling</u>

Training 4

2. The money <u>lying/found</u> in the suitcase was stolen from Lloyds Bank.
   or: The money <u>stolen</u> from Lloyds Bank was found in a suitcase.
3. The girl <u>sitting</u> on the bench is reading a book.
   or: The girl <u>reading</u> a book is sitting on a bench.
4. The letter <u>posted</u> on 12 August is lying on the desk.
   or: The letter <u>lying</u> on the desk was posted on 12 August.
5. The car <u>parked</u> in front of the house is from Britain.
   or: The car <u>registered</u> in Britain is/was parked in front of the house.
6. The languages <u>spoken</u> here are English, French and German.
7. The Queen is the woman <u>going</u> shopping at Harrods/into the store.
   or: The woman <u>going</u> shopping at Harrods/into the store is the Queen.
8. The woman <u>being interviewed</u> here is the actress Jane Jones.
   or: The actress Jane Jones is the woman <u>being interviewed</u> here.
9. "Hamlet" is the play <u>being put on/performed</u> at this theatre.
   or: The play <u>being put on/performed</u> at this theatre is "Hamlet".

Training 5

1. <u>Walking</u> across the room, I shut the door. — 2. <u>Having listened</u> to the new CD, we went out for a hamburger. — 3. <u>Not knowing</u> the way, he asked a passer-by. — 4. *No change.* — 5. Unless <u>taught</u> English properly, they will not be able to get good jobs abroad. — 6. Passengers <u>leaving</u> the train, should take all their luggage with them. — 7. Stay calm if <u>stopped</u> by a policeman. — 8. Though <u>made</u> in Korea, this car is still very good. — 9. *No change.* — 10. <u>Walking</u> into the room, the headmaster sat down at the teacher's table. — 11. *No change. or:* She had no worries until <u>told to leave</u> the country within 48 hours. — 12. John went to Oxford after <u>getting</u> four A's in his A-levels.

Training 6

1. <u>Shutting</u> the door, he sat down. — 2. <u>Having passed</u> my driving test, I bought a car. — 3. She sat in the bath <u>reading</u> a newspaper. – <u>(While) Sitting</u> in the bath she read a newspaper. — 4. <u>Not wanting</u> to go, we stayed at home. — 5. <u>Not having learnt</u> French at school, I wasn't able to read the letter. — 6. My friend fell asleep <u>(while) watching</u> TV. — 7. <u>Not living</u> in the area, she could not help me. — 8. Our dog ran off, <u>having bitten</u> the postman. *or:* <u>Having bitten</u> the postman, our dog ran off. — 9. <u>Being</u> foreigners, they had to learn English. — 10. <u>Walking</u> to school, I learn ten English words on the way. *or:* I walk to school <u>learning</u> ten English words on the way.

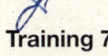

Training 7

1. She just sat there <u>watching</u> TV. — 2. The children went <u>running</u> down to the beach. — 3. The policemen just stood there <u>waiting</u> for orders. — 4. The food remained <u>untouched</u>. — 5. He spends a lot of time <u>dancing</u> in discos. — 6. The farmer caught two campers <u>camping</u> in his field without permission. — 7. They have wasted a lot of time <u>playing</u> football at the weekends. — 8. The sailor lay on the grass <u>drunk</u>. *or:* The sailor lay <u>drunk</u> on the grass. — 9. They spent a lot of time <u>sunbathing</u>. — 10. I can't stand here all day <u>waiting</u> for you! *or:* I can't stand here <u>waiting</u> for you all day!

Training 8

1. I saw/watched several people <u>waiting</u> for the bus.
   I saw/watched a street musician <u>playing</u> in the Underground.
   I saw/watched several people <u>looking</u> at the shop windows.
2. I watched the traffic <u>driving</u> up and down.
3. I listened to a street musician <u>playing</u> in the Underground.
   I listened to a police siren <u>wailing</u> in the distance.
4. I heard several people <u>speaking</u> German.
   I heard a police siren <u>wailing</u> in the distance.
   I heard a jet plane <u>break</u> the sound barrier.
5. I felt the hot sun <u>warming</u> the back of my neck.
   I felt a hand <u>touch</u> my shoulder. It was my good friend Bob …

Training 9

Gerund:
I like <u>living</u> in the big city. — <u>Working</u> as an archaeologist must be fun. — I wouldn't mind <u>studying</u> archaeology — I love <u>walking</u> around the streets of London — streets which you can only reach by <u>walking</u> through narrow alleys — I have got used to <u>hearing</u> the sound of traffic — I must stop <u>writing</u> now and start <u>doing</u> my homework. — but <u>living</u> near the centre of a town — I look forward to <u>seeing</u> you at Christmas.

Present participle:
London is a <u>living</u> museum! — <u>Sitting</u> on the upper deck of a bus — the high wooden fence <u>surrounding</u> a big building site. — As well as <u>building</u> workers — students <u>looking</u> for Roman remains — The mist <u>rising</u> from the lakes — I would find myself <u>writing</u> about a big city — But after <u>living</u> in London for nearly four weeks — the sound of traffic <u>rolling</u> through the city — <u>Waking</u> up at night — makes life so much more <u>interesting</u>

Progressive form:
<u>I've been living</u> in Central London

Training 10

1. Swimming is one of my hobbies. — 2. I like swimming in the sea. — 3. I soon got used to swimming in salt water. — 4. Swimming at the swimming baths is not as nice. — 5. I don't mind going to the/an open-air swimming pool at the weekend(s). — 6. My brother doesn't mind me/my going without him. — 7. Collecting old records/LPs is his favourite hobby. — 8. He finances/pays for his hobby by delivering news-papers. — 9. My mother doesn't like him/his having to deliver newspapers in bad weather. — 10. She is looking forward to him/his starting a proper job soon.

Training 11

1. living — 2. to remember; living — 3. moving — 4. to ask — 5. to give — 6. shop-ping — 7. to find; finding — 8. asking — 9. to talk —10. talking; telling — 11. leaving — 12. to live — 13. to mention — 14. to say

Kapitel 10

Einstufungstest

1c), 2a), 3a), 4b), 5d), 6c), 7b), 8a)

Training 1

Simple present:
Every year our rivers <u>are polluted</u> — that these sources of pollution <u>are</u> more strictly <u>inspected</u>! — to make sure that this trend <u>is stopped</u>! — No more nuclear power <u>is needed</u> in Britain! — In areas where local government <u>is taken</u> over or <u>supported</u> by

Simple past:
Last year 200,000 more private cars <u>were registered</u> — as many new jobs as <u>was expected</u>.

Present perfect:
very little <u>has been done</u> to reduce this amount. — Plans ... <u>have not been shelved</u> — Nothing <u>has been done</u> to improve — The standard of service <u>has</u> not <u>been improved</u>

Past perfect:
After an official report ... <u>had been requested</u> — even though many protests <u>had been made</u> — after they <u>had been closed</u> to passenger traffic

Auxiliary + infinitive:
When <u>will</u> this <u>be stopped</u>? — Solar or wind energy <u>should be developed</u> — Alternative sources of energy <u>will have to be found</u>! — Small local businesses <u>will be given</u> more support ... — more bus routes <u>will be provided</u> — railways ... <u>will be reopened</u>.

Progressive forms:
the problem <u>was being considered</u>. — Waste ... <u>is</u> still <u>being produced</u> — small factories <u>were</u> still <u>being closed down</u> — Even now, very little <u>is being done</u> — Only multinational companies ... <u>are being encouraged</u>

Training 2

1. we will be met at the airport. — 2. are opened. — 3. rooms were booked — 4. can be taken — 5. are made on Malta. — 6. were picked up — 7. are visited — 8. A coach trip can be taken — 9. may/can not be booked — 10. has been arranged

Training 3

1. is understood — 2. is real English spoken? — 3. tourists are disliked — 4. was stolen — 5. has been made — 6. hadn't been made — 7. we are liked

Training 4

1. A heavily-armed police riot squad <u>broke up</u> a peaceful demonstration in Trafalgar Square yesterday.— 2. Angry policemen <u>arrested</u> several (peaceful) demonstrators. — 3. After the riot squad <u>had been called</u>, probably by unnamed police informers, — 4. armour-plated police Land Rovers <u>brought</u> about twenty policemen in riot gear to Trafalgar Square. — 5. Bullying constables <u>ordered</u> Jessica Davies, the leader of the demonstration, to ask her fellow demonstrators to go home. — 6. Angry police armed with heavy sticks <u>took</u> one or two demonstrators to Marlborough Street police station. Police <u>kept</u> them there overnight because they refused to give their names. — 7. Ms Catherine Binyon, chairperson of PEACE NOW, <u>has not yet been released</u>. — 8. During the past few months our peaceful organization <u>has held</u> four demonstrations.

Training 5

a) 1. Industrial waste <u>is being discharged</u> into the river. — 2. Rubbish <u>is being dumped</u> in the woods/forests. — 3. Private cars <u>are not being used</u> efficiently. — 4. Valuable raw materials <u>are being thrown</u> away. — 5. Public transport <u>is not being used</u> enough — 6. A new hypermarket with a huge car park <u>is being built</u>. — 7. Railway stations <u>are being closed</u>./This railway station <u>is being closed</u> on 1st August. — 8. Gas-guzzlers <u>are</u> still <u>being developed</u>. — 9. Old paper and cardboard boxes <u>are not being recycled</u>. —10. Cigarette advertising <u>is</u> (still) <u>not being banned</u>.

b) *So könnte dein Artikel in etwa aussehen:*

A few weeks ago some of us carried out an Environmental Audit and this is what we discovered. Industrial waste <u>was</u> still <u>being discharged</u> into the river. We saw that rubbish <u>was</u> still <u>being dumped</u> in the woods near our school. When we checked the traffic driving into/out of our town/village one morning/afternoon, we noticed that private cars <u>were not being used</u> efficiently. There was usually only one person – the driver – in each car! Valuable raw materials such as tins, cans and bottles <u>were being thrown</u> away despite the many recycling containers and bottle banks in our town/village. The buses were often almost empty because public transport <u>was not being used</u> (enough). Despite protests and demonstrations a/the new hypermarket with a large/big/huge car park <u>was being built</u> on a green-field site on the edge of town/the village. We realized that public transport was being reduced still further when we saw that our local railway (station) <u>was being closed</u> (down) on 1st August. A report in the newspaper showed that gas-guzzlers <u>were</u> still <u>being developed</u> by the big multi-national automakers. We do not need these monsters and the extra pollution which their exhaust fumes produce! Old paper and cardboard boxes <u>were not being recycled</u> even though there are regular collections. Hoardings in the streets and advertisements in magazines clearly show that cigarette advertising <u>was</u> (still) <u>not being banned</u> as comprehensively as the Government has been promising. A health warning on the cigarette packet is not enough!

Training 6

"Nothing <u>is being done</u> about air pollution (by the present Government). Two new by-passes and another twenty miles of motorway <u>are being built</u> in my constituency alone! Last year they promised to halt construction of a nuclear power station which <u>was being planned</u>, but nothing <u>has been done</u>, and land near the River Don <u>is</u> already <u>being surveyed</u> in preparation for construction of this power station which <u>is</u> not <u>wanted</u>! The rivers in this beautiful part of Britain <u>are</u> still <u>being polluted</u>. Last year chemicals factories <u>were</u> still <u>being expanded</u> even though an enquiry into chemical pollution <u>had been promised</u>!"

Training 7 *(Einige Lösungsvorschläge):*

1. This book <u>was written</u> by a famous author/an Englishman.
2. Thatched houses <u>are not built</u> in Britain any longer.
3. Live music <u>is</u> often <u>played/is being played</u> here/in this pub/<u>was being played</u> here last week.
4. Good sandwiches <u>are made/sold</u> in this snack bar.
5. Excellent fruit <u>is grown</u> by these farmers/on this farm.
6. Gas-guzzlers <u>are/were</u> still <u>being built/made</u> by some car companies/<u>are</u> still <u>not banned</u> by the government.
7. The environment <u>is</u> still <u>being polluted</u> with chemicals/by some big firms.
8. Young people <u>are (being) trained</u> as doctors.
9. Many souvenirs <u>are made/sold</u> here every year.
10. Spanish <u>is spoken</u> in Spain/many countries of South and Central America.

Training 8

1. More industrial waste <u>is being dumped</u> in our rivers than ever before — 2. Prince William <u>was being followed</u> by 10 photographers yesterday — 3. The Nobel peace prize <u>has been awarded</u> to a dog! — 4. A famous film star <u>is being divorced</u> by her fifth husband — 5. Good marks <u>have been "sold"</u> to pupils (by a teacher) for years — 6. Foreign aid money <u>has been spent</u> on arms — 7. Drugs <u>were taken</u> by champion runner — 8. Traffic in northern Scotland <u>is being stopped</u> by 3 metres of snow — 9. Baby seals <u>have been killed</u> again (by hunters) — 10. Pop star Sam Brown's next concert <u>will be cancelled</u> — 11. A dog <u>has been bitten</u> by a man — 12. Many parts of Britain <u>are being flooded</u> (by heavy rain)

Training 9

1. Plenty <u>is being done</u>! — 2. The problem <u>is being looked into</u> at this very moment! — 3. I don't care what <u>is being worked out</u> by your cousin's firm — 4. A traffic-free zone <u>will/is going to be set up</u> as soon as — 5. More people <u>are knocked down</u> and injured — 6. who <u>would be locked up</u>! — 7. You mean this matter <u>has been/was talked about</u> at a meeting — 8. the matter <u>was brought up</u> at the end of the meeting — 9. I think the pavements <u>are being obstructed</u> by all those cars! — 10. It's not a bigger car park that <u>is needed</u> — 11. Bikes can't <u>be towed away</u>! — 12. But bikes have to <u>be chained up</u>! ... Thirty bikes <u>have been stolen</u> already this year!

Training 10

1. <u>I was handed</u> the note. — 2. <u>I have</u> never <u>been offered</u> a ride in her car! — 3. <u>Weren't you sent</u> an invitation to his party? — 4. <u>Haven't you been taught</u> to say please if you want something? — 5. <u>You won't be told</u> the truth. — 6. <u>We are being denied</u> our basic rights! — 7. <u>I was being given</u> an injection when the lights went out.

— 8. <u>She is going to be awarded</u> first prize in the photographic competition. — 9. <u>I haven't been shown</u> the photos yet. — 10. <u>This bike wasn't stolen./It was sold</u> to me. — 11. <u>She was promised</u> a new skateboard for Christmas. — 12. <u>I have been left</u> £5,000 by my great-grandfather/in my great-grandfather's will.

Training 11

20.4.04

1. This parcel <u>was delivered</u> to the wrong address. — 2. This problem <u>can't be explained</u> to people who know nothing about cricket. — 3. They <u>have not been introduced</u> to the President yet. — 4. The scenery <u>can</u> only <u>be described</u> to you with the help of these photos. — 5. The following solution <u>is proposed</u> to you. — 6. After the experiment <u>had been demonstrated</u> (to the chemistry teacher's/the pupils), the laboratory was full of smoke. — 7. The results of the elections <u>were announced</u> to the angry crowd. — 8. Nothing <u>was said</u> about this to me. — 9. Clothes <u>are being distributed</u> to the refugees. —10. An alternative <u>was suggested</u> to the worried workers.

Training 12

1. We <u>had been told</u> that our bank was robbery-proof. — 2. The alarm system <u>was said to be</u> perfect. ... — 3. The bank's security arrangements <u>are</u> now <u>felt to have been</u> inadequate. — 4. The robbers <u>are believed to have been hiding</u> in the bank all night. We <u>were surprised</u> when we arrived for work. — 5. We <u>were told to put up</u> our hands. — 6. Then we <u>were made to lie</u> down on the floor. — 7. The gang <u>is supposed to be</u> the same one that robbed the National Westminster Bank in Croydon last month. — 8. These men <u>are known to be</u> dangerous criminals! — 9. We <u>were told</u> not to move for ten minutes —10. because other crooks <u>were said to be</u> outside, watching in case the alarm <u>was given</u>. — 11. The robbers <u>were seen to leave</u> (the bank) in a fast car. — 12. When they had gone the manager, Mr Simms, <u>was found to have had</u> a mild heart-attack!

Kapitel 11

Einstufungstest

1b), 2d), 3b), 4b), 5c), 6d), 7d), 8a), 9b), 10a)

Training 1

List One – Modal auxiliaries:
This Evacuation Order <u>must</u> be observed — (persons) <u>should</u> apply to the Commanding Officer — who <u>may</u> be able to help. — Residents <u>must</u> take all their

furniture — No exceptions <u>can</u> be made — The general public <u>may</u> only visit — people <u>must not</u> leave the roads — because they <u>might</u> be injured — that the Army <u>ought to</u> keep its promise and <u>should</u> return Imber to the people

List Two – Substitutes:
Imber <u>is to be</u> evacuated on 1st December 1943. — Any persons who <u>are not able to</u> find accommodation — no one <u>will be allowed to</u> return — Residents <u>will be able to</u> return — the last 150 residents … <u>had to</u> leave their homes — They <u>were allowed to</u> take their possessions — but <u>were forbidden</u> (= not allowed) <u>to</u> return to the village — only St Giles Church … and a few buildings <u>have been allowed to</u> remain

List Three – Other tense-forming auxiliaries:
The beautiful old church <u>is</u> only used once a year. — The Army <u>has</u> built its own ugly buildings — NOTICE <u>is</u> hereby given … — From 2nd December 1943, all roads … <u>will</u> be CLOSED … — No exceptions <u>can</u> be made to this Order, which <u>is</u> issued in the interests of National Security. — They … <u>were</u> forbidden to return to the village.

Training 2

1. "<u>Must</u> we take all our animals with us?" – "Yes, you<u>'ll have to</u> take all your animals with you." — 2. "<u>May/Can</u> we come to church on Sundays?" – "I'm afraid you <u>won't be allowed/able to</u> come to church on Sundays." — 3. "<u>Couldn't</u> we possibly stay until the spring?" – "No you <u>won't be able to</u> stay until the spring." — 4. "<u>Can/May</u> we travel in one of your lorries?" – "Of course you<u>'ll be able/allowed to</u> travel in one of our lorries." — 5. "<u>Can't</u> we leave in one of your tanks?" – "Sorry, but you <u>won't be able to</u> leave in one of our tanks." *or:* "<u>May</u> we leave in one of your tanks?" – "Sorry, but you <u>won't be allowed to</u> leave in one of our tanks." — 6. "<u>Can/May</u> we take our rabbits?" – "Yes, you<u>'ll be able/allowed to</u> take your rabbits." — 7. "<u>Can/May</u> we take our hay?" – "No, you <u>won't be able to</u> take your hay." — 8. "<u>Couldn't</u> we bring our sheep back in summer?" – "No, you <u>won't be able/allowed to</u> bring your sheep back in summer." — 9. "<u>May</u> we borrow a few big wooden boxes (from you)?" – "Of course you <u>may</u> borrow a few big wooden boxes from us." — 10. "<u>Must</u> we lock our houses?" – "No, you <u>needn't</u> lock your houses."

Training 3

1. Do we have — 2. needn't — 3. mustn't — 4. had; I'll/will have — 5. has/will have/is having — 6. We've/have had — 7. Why have you had — 8. needn't — 9. must

Training 4

1. will be able to — 2. weren't able to — 3. have to — 4. needn't — 5. needn't; must/do — 6. has never had — 7. were able — 8. have never been able — 9. to be able to —10. will have to — 11. to be able to — 12. would be able — 13. hadn't been able to — 14. can't/haven't been able to — 15. will have to

Training 5

1. be allowed — 2. be allowed to — 3. may not — 4. may not — 5. was allowed — 6. may — 7. we'll be allowed — 8. Were you allowed — 9. weren't allowed — 10. May — 11. Might — 12. might — 13. may — 14. might — 15. may/might

Training 6

1. "May I borrow your book?" — 2. "Might I possibly use your/your father's computer?" — 3. "I think this £5 note may be a forgery." — 4. "I think you might be too young to watch the horror video with me." — 5."We may take/have a holiday in Spain next year." — 6. "If we had more money we might take/have a holiday on Hawaii." — 7. "You may not borrow my Rolls Royce!" — 8. "I don't think we will be allowed to go alone." — 9. "If my brother went with us I think I would be allowed to go to the pop concert in Edinburgh next week." — 10. "You may be right." — 11."It might be right/wrong." — 12. "… At home I've always been allowed to watch my favourite programme (on TV)!"

Training 7

1. "Shall we go for a bike-ride in the country?" — 2. "Perhaps we should take our rain capes with us." — 3. "Perhaps we oughtn't to/shouldn't go too far." — 4. "The little lake on the edge of the forest is said to be good for swimming." — 5. "Hey! You oughtn't to/shouldn't cycle on the left-hand side in Germany!" — 6. "I ought to know that by now!" — 7. "It's supposed/said to be haunted." — 8. "Shall we have a look around?" — 9. "That sign means nobody is supposed to go inside the house." — 10. "Perhaps we oughtn't to/shouldn't/we'd better not go in, then." — 11. "Yes, if anyone/someone were to see us we might get into trouble." — 12. "I think we should/ought to/we'd better go home before it gets dark."

Training 8

1. "Do you wish/want to speak to me, Headmaster? — 2. "Oh, Karin! Yes. I was going/wanted/intended to phone you this morning." — 3. "Why?" – "I was going to/wanted to ask you if you would like to take part in our Class Excursion/Trip." — 4. "I really intended/meant to stay at home at the weekend. — 5. My aunt wants/is going/intends/(means) to visit us." — 6. They wanted/intended to see the film, but did not want/intend to queue for tickets. — 7. "What do you intend/are you going to do with the money?" — 8. "I'm going to buy a mountain bike. — 9. I've always wanted to have a mountain bike."